# Fathers Are Forever

# Fathers Are Forever

Quotations Honoring the
Wisest Men We Know

*Compiled and Edited by Criswell Freeman*

WALNUT GROVE PRESS
Nashville, TN 37205

ISBN 1-887655-77-8

*The ideas expressed in this book are not, in all cases, exact quotations, as some have been edited for clarity and brevity. In all cases, the author has attempted to maintain the speaker's original intent. In some cases, material for this book was obtained from secondary sources, primarily print media. While every effort was made to ensure the accuracy of these sources, the accuracy cannot be guaranteed. For additions, deletions, corrections or clarifications in future editions of this text, please write WALNUT GROVE PRESS.*

Printed in the United States of America
Typesetting & Page Layout by Sue Gerdes
Editor for Walnut Grove Press: Alan Ross
2 3 4 5 6 7 8 9 10 • 98 99 00 01 02

ACKNOWLEDGMENTS
The author gratefully acknowledges the helpful support of Angela Freeman, Dick and Mary Freeman, and Mary Susan Freeman.

*For Dad*

# Table of Contents

# Introduction

You hold in your hands a simple tribute to fathers. On the pages herein, you will examine the attributes of dynamic dads and peerless pops. You will consider the considerable skills of fabulous fathers and great granddads. And you will discover a heaping helping of fatherly advice.

This collection of quotations celebrates the paternal side of parenting, and with good cause. Fathers bequeath a timeless legacy — one that is passed from generation to generation. The hand that rocks the cradle also places its handprint upon eternity.

If you happen to be a father, and since you're reading this book there is a high probability that you are, congratulations and thank you. In touching the lives of your children and their friends, you have left the world a better place. Your handiwork will last forever.

# 1

# A Father Is...

The dictionary defines the word father as "a male parent," but every grateful son or daughter knows that definition to be woefully incomplete. A good father is many things: He is a leader, a provider, an advisor, a disciplinarian, a teacher, a recreation director, a friend, a spiritual guide, a babysitter, a transportation director, a handyman and a banker.

To a young child, a father is an all-purpose, all-powerful, all-knowing figure. As the child matures, the father's image may tarnish — temporarily. But the adult child, armed with a better understanding of the demands of parenthood, is likely to appreciate the father more than ever. And rightly so.

On the pages that follow, we consider the wide-ranging implications of fatherhood, a job so demanding and so important that God reserved it for dads.

No music is so pleasant to my ears as that word — father.

*Lydia Maria Child*

The father is always a Republican toward
his son, and his mother's always a Democrat.

*Robert Frost*

A father is the man who expects his son
to be as good as the man he meant to be.

*Franklin A. Clark*

One father equals a hundred schoolmasters.

*George Herbert*

You don't have to deserve your mother's love.
You have to deserve your father's.
He's more particular.

*Robert Frost*

Children's children are the crown of old men;
the glory of children are their fathers.

*Proverbs 17:6*

Tell me who your father is and I'll tell you
who you are.

*Philippine Proverb*

When I was a boy of 14,
my father was so ignorant
I could hardly stand to
have the old man around.
But when I got to be 21,
I was astonished at how
much the old man had
learned in seven years.

*Mark Twain*

My only major influence
was my father. He had
power. Everything was
done around his presence,
even when he wasn't
there.

*Jane Fonda*

# Have we not all one father? Did not one God create us?

*Malachi 2:10*

You are a king by your own fireside,
    as much as any monarch in his thrown.

*Miguel de Cervantes*

A father is a banker provided by nature.

*French Proverb*

A father is a man who can't get on the phone,
    in the bathroom, or out of the house.

*Anonymous*

# 2

# Family

Sam Levenson joked, "Insanity is hereditary, you can get it from your kids." Spoken like a man with a big family. The philosopher George Santayana wrote, "A family is a masterpiece of nature." In this chapter, we consider that masterpiece … and its master.

It takes a heap of lovin'
in a house to make
it a home.

*Edgar A. Guest*

A family is a place where principles
are hammered and honed on the anvil
of everyday living.

*Charles R. Swindoll*

A happy family is but an earlier heaven.

*Sir John Bowring*

Better a hundred enemies outside
the house than one inside.

*Arabian Proverb*

Other things may change us, but we start
and end with the family.

*Anthony Brandt*

A family is a unit composed not only of children, but of men, women, an occasional animal, and the common cold.

*Ogden Nash*

A family is the we of me.

*Carson McCullers*

You don't choose your family. They are
God's gift to you, as you are to them.
*Desmond Tutu*

There are three partners in any man:
God, his father, and his mother.
*Old Saying*

The most important thing a father can do
for his children is to love their mother.
*Rev. Theodore M. Hesburgh*

A child is the greatest poem ever known.
*Christopher Morley*

Blessed indeed is the man who hears many
gentle voices call him father!
*Lydia Maria Child*

A family is the school of duties founded on love.

*Felix Adler*

A family is the first
and essential cell
of human society.

*Pope John XXIII*

# When the family is together, the soul is at peace.

*Russian Proverb*

*Family*

A large family gives beauty to the house.

*Indian Proverb*

As is the family, so are the offspring.

*Russian Proverb*

A family divided against itself
        will perish together.

*Indian Proverb*

The family you come from isn't as important
        as the family you're going to have.

*Ring Lardner*

Father and mother are the most precious
        jewels on earth.

*Philippine Proverb*

# Whoever is ashamed of his family will have no luck.

*Yiddish Proverb*

*Family*

A baby is God's opinion that the world
should go on.

*Carl Sandburg*

The family is the nucleus of civilization.

*Will and Ariel Durant*

A child is a beam of sunlight from
the Infinite and Eternal.

*Lyman Abbott*

The best things you can give children next
to good habits, are good memories.

*Sydney J. Harris*

A torn jacket is soon mended,
but hard words bruise the heart of a child.

*Henry Wadsworth Longfellow*

# Children have more need of models than critics.

*Joseph Joubert*

*Family*

It is a wise father that knows his own child.

*William Shakespeare*

A good father will leave his imprint
on his daughter for the rest of her life.

*James C. Dobson*

A father's interest in having a child —
perhaps his only child — may be unmatched
by any other interest in his life.

*William H. Rehnquist*

About his children every parent is blind.

*Old Saying*

Build me a son, O Lord, who will be strong
enough to know when he is weak and brave
enough to face himself when he is afraid.

*Douglas MacArthur*

When a father complains that his son has
taken to evil ways, what should he do?
Love him more than ever.

*Ba'al Shem Tov*

They say the best product off a farm
is the children.

*Earl Simpson*

In a big family, the first child is kind of like
the first pancake. If it's not perfect, that's
okay, there are a lot more coming along.

*Antonin Scalia*

All children alarm their parents,
if only because you are forever expecting
to encounter yourself.

*Gore Vidal*

When a father helps a son, both smile;
when a son must help his father, both cry.

*Old Jewish Saying*

*Family*

A king, realizing his incompetence, can
either delegate or abdicate his duties.
A father can do neither. If only sons could see
the paradox, they would understand
the dilemma.

*Marlene Dietrich*

America's future will be determined by the
home and the school. The child becomes
largely what he is taught; hence we must watch
what we teach and how we live.

*Jane Addams*

When I met Michael Jordan I wondered how,
with all the distractions, he could maintain
such mountains of freshness. Then I met his
family and I understood. It sounds corny,
but it's true — love shows.

*Doug Collins*

Lucky is that man whose children make
his happiness in life.

*Euripides*

What we desire our children to become,
we must endeavor to be before them.

*Andrew Combe*

Our sages recommended that a father
should spend less than his means on food,
up to his means on dress, and beyond
his means for his wife and children.

*Maimonides*

It is not enough for parents to understand
children. They must accord children the
privilege of understanding *them.*

*Milton R. Sapirstein*

A strict master will not have
understanding sons.

*Nachman of Bratslav*

It is better to keep children to their duty by a
sense of honor and by kindness than by fear.

*Terence*

My mother gave me my religious training
and my respect for discipline. My father supplied the athletic genes. There is nothing that I
am today that I would be without family.

*Emmitt Smith*

A man cannot leave a better legacy
to the world than a well-educated family.

*Thomas Scott*

Here all mankind is equal: rich and poor alike,
they love their children.

*Euripides*

Children are the hands by which we take
hold of heaven.

*Henry Ward Beecher*

# Govern a family as you would cook a small fish — very gently.

*Chinese Proverb*

*Family*

The debt of gratitude we owe our mother
and father goes forward, not backward.
What we owe our parents is the bill presented
to us by our children.

*Nancy Friday*

Raising children is not unlike a long distance
race in which the contestants must learn
to pace themselves. That is the secret
of winning.

*James C. Dobson*

Honor your father-in-law and mother-in-law,
for now they are your parents.

*Tobit*

There is no grandfather who does not adore
his grandson.

*Victor Hugo*

The father in praising the son extols himself.

*Chinese Proverb*

When brothers agree, no fortress
 is so strong as their common life.
*Antisthenes*

The voice of parents is the voice of gods, for
to their children they are heaven's lieutenants.
*William Shakespeare*

Through the survival of their children,
 happy parents are able to think calmly, and
 with a very practical affection, of a world in
 which they are to have no direct share.
*Walter Pater*

Nobody's family can hang out the sign:
 Nothing the Matter Here.
*Chinese Proverb*

Upon our children — how they are taught —
rests the fate, or fortune, of tomorrow's world.
*B. C. Forbes*

Examine yourselves —
ask, each of you,
"Have I been a good
brother? ... son? ...
husband? ... father? ...
servant?"

*Charles Kingsley*

# 3

# Fatherly Advice

A hundred years before the birth of Christ, Publilius Syrus observed, "Many receive advice, few profit from it." For twenty-one centuries, fathers everywhere have known exactly how he felt.

In a 1955 television interview, Harry Truman commented, "I have always found the best way to give advice to your children is to find out what they want and then advise them to do it." Obviously, President Truman spoke from experience. No matter how sound a father's recommendations, his child seems compelled to do it "my way." Contrary advice usually falls upon deaf ears.

In this chapter, we consider an assortment of helpful hints that fathers everywhere might be proud to share — and kids everywhere might be likely to ignore.

Advice is a sacred thing.

*Plato*

No one wants advice — only corroboration.

*John Steinbeck*

We may give advice, but we cannot
inspire conduct.

*La Rochefoucauld*

# My son, hear the instruction of thy father.

*Proverbs 1: 8*

Whoever teaches his son
teaches not only his son
but also his son's son.

*Talmud*

In our family, we try to make something happen rather than wait around for it to happen.

*James Jordan, Michael Jordan's father*

My grandfather always said that living is like licking honey off a thorn.

*Louis Adamic*

Every morning at our house we had squats and sit-ups 15 minutes before breakfast. My father used to say, "First you have to earn your breakfast."

*Arnold Schwarzenegger*

The only thing Dad ever told me was to go out and have fun. Whatever happens happens. Stay out of trouble and be a good kid.

*Ken Griffey, Jr.*

Bitterness imprisons life, love releases it.
*Harry Emerson Fosdick*

Scatter seeds of kindness.
*George Ade*

No act of kindness, no matter how small,
is ever wasted.
*Aesop*

Look upon the errors of others in sorrow,
not in anger.
*Henry Wadsworth Longfellow*

Life is an exercise in forgiveness.
*Norman Cousins*

The jealous are troublesome to others
but a torment to themselves.

*William Penn*

Jealousy is a mental cancer.

*B. C. Forbes*

Don't lose faith in humanity: Think of all
the people in the United States who have
never played you a single nasty trick.

*Elbert Hubbard*

The only way to have a friend is to be one.

*Ralph Waldo Emerson*

If you can't stand yourself,
neither can anybody else!

*Sid Caesar*

People ought to do what comes easy for them. Too many struggle with things that are difficult for them and that they have no business trying to do.

*George Bernard Shaw*

Work is a grand cure of all the maladies that ever beset mankind.

*Thomas Carlyle*

Blessed is the man who has found his work.

*Elbert Hubbard*

People who suffer in unsatisfying jobs are assuming the victim role. Nothing is going to help them if they don't help themselves.

*Bernie Siegel, M.D.*

Work and save.

*Bernard Baruch*

If there is no wind, row.

*Latin Proverb*

The secret of a long life is double careers.
One to about age 60, then another
for the next 30 years.

*David Ogilvy*

Work as if you were to live 100 years;
pray as if you were to die tomorrow.

*Ben Franklin*

Genius is nothing but a greater aptitude
for patience.

*Ben Franklin*

If you only keep adding little by little,
it will soon become a big heap.

*Hesiod*

All good abides with him
who waiteth wisely.

*Henry David Thoreau*

No great thing is created suddenly.

*Epictetus*

Here is the test to find
whether your mission
on earth is finished:
If you're alive, it isn't.

*Richard Bach*

The best place to get help is from yourself.

*Epictetus*

One thorn of experience is worth
a whole wilderness of warning.

*James Russell Lowell*

Never wait for trouble.

*Charles "Chuck" Yeager*

The time will come when winter will ask
what you were doing all summer.

*Henry Clay*

# Never take away hope from any human being.

*Oliver Wendell Holmes, Sr.*

*Fatherly Advice*

Rudeness is the weak man's imitation
of strength.

*Eric Hoffer*

You can't hold a man down without staying
down with him.

*Booker T. Washington*

Conscience is the perfect interpreter of life.

*Karl Barth*

If you tell the truth, you don't have
to remember anything.

*Mark Twain*

Every charitable act is a stepping-stone
toward heaven.

*Henry Ward Beecher*

# We are not punished for our sins, but by them.

*Elbert Hubbard*

Always keep your word.
A gentleman never insults
anyone intentionally.
Don't look for trouble, but
if you get into a fight,
make sure you win it.

*Clyde Morrison, John Wayne's Father*

When you're green, you're growing. When you're ripe, you rot.

*Ray Kroc*

# Honor thy father and mother.

*Exodus 20:12*

# 4

# Courage

Thoughtful fathers teach the importance of courage and character, knowing that their children will then pass along the message to future generations. But the teaching process requires more than words; morality lessons, like all paternal preachments, are best taught by example.

Heraclitus observed, "A man's fate is his character." He might have added that a father's character often contributes to the fate of his children. The following quotations remind us that character pays big dividends — now, and for generations to come.

Courage is the first of human qualities
because it is the quality which guarantees
all the others.

*Sir Winston Churchill*

Courage is always the surest wisdom.

*Sir Wilfred Grenfell*

When there is no money, half is gone;
when there is no courage, all is gone.

*Old Jewish Saying*

Courage is grace under pressure.

*Ernest Hemingway*

One man with courage
is a majority.

*Andrew Jackson*

Discontent is want of self-reliance.
>> *Ralph Waldo Emerson*

Courage is resistance to fear,
>> mastery of fear — not absence of fear.
>> *Mark Twain*

We must have courage to bet on our ideas,
>> to take the calculated risk, and to act.
>> Everyday living requires courage if life
>> is to be effective and bring happiness.
>> *Maxwell Maltz*

The only courage that matters is the kind
>> that gets you from one moment to the next.
>> *Mignon McLaughlin*

Nerve succeeds.

*Old Jewish Saying*

Courage is contagious.
When a brave man takes a stand, the spines
of others are often stiffened.

*Billy Graham*

When you're afraid, keep your mind on
what you have to do. And if you have been
thoroughly prepared, you will not be afraid.

*Dale Carnegie*

They conquer who believe they can.

*John Dryden*

Character is that which can do
without success.

*Ralph Waldo Emerson*

Character is what you are in the dark.

*Dwight L. Moody*

Character is higher than intellect.

*Ralph Waldo Emerson*

When you have no choice, at least be brave.

*Old Saying*

Fear corrupts.

*John Steinbeck*

Even if fear can act as a good advisor,
there is no use cultivating it. In the long run
it can only hurt you.

*Luciano Pavarotti*

Do the thing you fear and the death of fear
is certain.

*Ralph Waldo Emerson*

Where is the university for courage?
The university for courage is to do
what you believe in!

*El Cordobés, world-renowned Spanish matador*

You don't raise heroes, you raise sons. And if you treat them like sons, they'll turn out to be heroes, even if it's just in your own eyes.

*Walter M. Schirra, Sr.*

When you get to the end of your rope, tie a knot and hang on.

*Franklin D. Roosevelt*

# 5

# Happiness

A father seeks happiness for his children but cannot force it upon them. Ultimately, each child must bear the responsibility for his own peace of mind — or lack of it. Robert Louis Stevenson observed, "There is no duty so much underrated as the duty of being happy." If you've been neglecting your duties, consider the advice that follows; your dad is counting on you.

To live we must conquer incessantly; we must have the courage to be happy.

*Henri Frédéric Amiel*

Happiness comes of the capacity to feel
deeply, to enjoy simply, to think freely,
to risk life, to be needed.

*Storm Jameson*

Happiness is when what you think,
what you say, and what you do are in harmony.

*Mohandas Gandhi*

Happiness is something you get
as a by-product in the process
of making something else.

*Aldous Huxley*

Everyone chases after happiness,
not noticing that happiness is at their heels.

*Bertolt Brecht*

An inexhaustible good nature is one
of the most precious gifts of heaven.

*Washington Irving*

Mirth is better than fun, and happiness is
better than mirth.

*William Blake*

Humor is the best therapy.

*Norman Cousins*

He is the happiest, be he king or peasant,
who finds peace in his home.

*Goethe*

# A good laugh is sunshine in a house.

*William Makepeace Thackeray*

I am happy and content because I think I am.
*Alain-René Lesage*

Happiness is a habit. Cultivate it.
*Elbert Hubbard*

Happiness and misery depend as much
on temperament as on fortune.
*La Rochefoucauld*

The happiness of your life depends upon
the character of your thoughts.
*Marcus Aurelius*

A man should so live that his happiness
shall depend as little as possible
on external things.
*Epictetus*

Happiness depends,
as Nature shows,
Less on exterior things
than most suppose.

*William Cowper*

The U.S. Constitution doesn't guarantee
happiness, only the pursuit of it.
You have to catch up with it yourself.

*Ben Franklin*

When a man has lost all happiness,
he's not alive. Call him a breathing corpse.

*Sophocles*

To fill the hour and leave no crevice —
that is happiness.

*Ralph Waldo Emerson*

Happiness in this world, when it comes, comes incidentally. Make it the object of pursuit, and it leads us on a wild-goose chase and is never attained. Follow some other object, and very possibly we may find that we have caught happiness without dreaming of it.

*Nathaniel Hawthorne*

Happiness means having something to do and something to live for.

*Bishop Fulton J. Sheen*

Happiness to me means constant growth.

*Eddie Albert*

Men are made for happiness, and anyone who is completely happy has a right to say to himself: "I am doing God's will on earth."

*Anton Chekhov*

# Don't mistake pleasures for happiness.

*Josh Billings*

To do without some of the things you want
is an indispensable part of happiness.

*Bertrand Russell*

Before we set our hearts too much on
anything, let us examine how happy are those
who already possess it.

*La Rochefoucauld*

Be content with such things as ye have.

*Hebrews 13:5*

People with many interests live
      not only longest, but happiest.

*George Matthew Allen*

Make the work interesting and the discipline
      will take care of itself.

*E. B. White*

Never is work without reward
      or reward without work.

*Livy*

Give a man health and a course to steer
and he'll never stop to trouble about whether
      he's happy or not.

*George Bernard Shaw*

Get happiness out of your work, or you may
      never know what happiness is.

*Elbert Hubbard*

Choose a job you love,
and you will never work
a day in your life.

*Confucius*

Happiness? That's nothing more than health and a poor memory.

*Albert Schweitzer*

# 6

# Faith

Clement of Alexandria, the great Greek theologian, observed, "Faith is the ear of the soul." He might have added that, when it comes to the spiritual ear, most of us suffer from occasional bouts of hearing loss. From time to time, we all fall prey to fits of depression, pessimism or doubt. Even fathers are not immune. But perceptive pops understand that when life gets tough, it's time to turn up the spiritual hearing aid.

No matter how big the problem, faith is the answer. Leo Tolstoy grasped this fact when he wrote, "Faith is the force of life." Hear, hear.

The greatest asset of a man, a business,
or a nation, is faith.

*Thomas J. Watson*

Entertain great hopes.

*Robert Frost*

All work that is worth anything is done
in faith.

*Albert Schweitzer*

Belief is a truth held in the mind.
Faith is a fire in the heart.

*Joseph Fort Newton*

Faith can give us courage to face
the uncertainties of the future.

*Martin Luther King, Jr.*

Faith is the daring of the soul to go farther
than it can see.

*William Newton Clark*

The man without faith is a walking corpse.

*Pope Xystus I*

Treat the other man's faith gently;
it is all he has to believe with.

*Henry S. Haskins*

Faith is building on what
you know is here, so you
can reach what you know
is there.

*Cullen Hightower*

It is impossible on
reasonable grounds to
disbelieve miracles.

*Blaise Pascal*

Faith is knowing with your heart.

*N. Richard Nash*

Understanding is the reward of faith.
Therefore seek not to understand that thou
mayest believe, but believe that thou
mayest understand.

*St. Augustine*

Faith is the substance of things hoped for,
the evidence of things not seen.

*Hebrews 11:1*

Faith is a higher facility than reason.

*Philip James Bailey*

Faith is reason grown courageous.

*Sherwood Eddy*

Hope is an adventure, a going forward —
a confident search for a rewarding life.

*Karl Menninger*

Deep faith eliminates fear.

*Lech Walesa*

They can conquer who believe they can.

*Ralph Waldo Emerson*

Faith means belief in something,concerning which doubt is theoretically possible.

*William James*

No faith is our own that we have not arduously won.

*Havelock Ellis*

Faith, as an intellectual state, is self-reliance.

*Oliver Wendell Holmes, Sr.*

Hope deferred maketh the heart sick.

*Proverbs 13:12*

Some things have to be believed to be seen.

*Ralph Hodgson*

Make no little plans. They have no magic to stir men's blood. Make big plans: Aim high in hope and work hard.

*Daniel Hudson Burnham*

All human wisdom is
summed up in two words:
wait and hope.

*Alexandre Dumas*

# 7

# Hard Work

The Book of Ecclesiastes tells us that "Hard work is the lot of every man." It might be added that the lot of most fathers is *very* hard work. But thoughtful dads don't just bring home the bacon; they teach their children to do the same.

Leonardo da Vinci observed, "God sells us all things at the price of labor." Hard-working fathers understand exactly what he meant. And they teach their children that the key to success is a willingness to pay the price.

*Hard Work*

All work is as seed sown; it grows and
spreads and sows itself anew.

*Thomas Carlyle*

The procrastinating man is ever struggling
with ruin.

*Hesiod*

A journey of a thousand miles begins
with one step.

*Lao-tzu*

Make it a point to do something every day
that you don't want to do. This is the golden
rule for acquiring the habit of doing your duty
without pain.

*Mark Twain*

Everything comes to him who hustles
while he waits.

*Thomas Alva Edison*

Everywhere in life, the true question is not what we gain, but what we do.

*Thomas Carlyle*

The test of any man lies in action.

*Pindar*

To dispose a soul to action, we must upset
its equilibrium.

*Eric Hoffer*

For purposes of action, nothing is more useful
than narrowness of thought combined with
energy of will.

*Henri Frédéric Amiel*

He who considers too much
will perform little.

*Schiller*

Knowing is not enough, we must apply;
willing is not enough, we must do.

*Goethe*

The great end of life
is not knowledge
but action.

*Thomas Huxley*

Our main business is not to see what lies
dimly at a distance, but to do what lies
clearly at hand.

*Thomas Carlyle*

Do noble things, do not dream them
all day long.

*Charles Kingsley*

To work is to pray.

*Benedictine Motto*

If you can dream it, you can do it.

*Walt Disney*

Shallow men believe in luck. Strong men
believe in cause and effect.

*Ralph Waldo Emerson*

Peace in this life springs from acquiescence to,
not an exemption from, suffering.

*François de Fénelon*

The world cares very little about what a man
or woman knows; it is what the man or woman
is able to do that counts.

*Booker T. Washington*

Act well at the moment, and you have
performed a good action for all eternity.

*Johann K. Lavater*

Work and love — these are the basics.

*Theodor Reik*

Well done is better than well said.

*Ben Franklin*

God gives every bird its food, but he does not throw it into the nest.

*Josiah Gilbert Holland*

Live truth instead of professing it.

*Elbert Hubbard*

By their fruits ye shall know them.

*Matthew 7:20*

Hell is to drift. Heaven is to steer.

*George Bernard Shaw*

One must act in painting as in life — directly.

*Pablo Picasso*

To win one's joy through struggle is better
than to yield to melancholy.

*André Gide*

It is faith, and not reason, which impels men
to action. Intelligence is content to point out
the road but never drives us along it.

*Dr. Alexis Carrel*

To think is easy, to act is difficult;
to act as one thinks is most difficult of all.

*Goethe*

Do what you can with what you have
where you are.

*Theodore Roosevelt*

Elbow grease is the best polish.

*English Proverb*

Luck is the residue of design.

*Branch Rickey*

Learn how to fail intelligently.

*Charles F. Kettering*

Do everything. One thing may turn out right.

*Humphrey Bogart*

# 8

# Peace of Mind

In the first century before the birth of Jesus, Publilius Syrus noted, "An angry father is most cruel toward himself." In the intervening twenty-one centuries, absolutely nothing has changed. When a father loses his temper, he instantly becomes his own worst enemy. Unfortunately, the pressures of fatherhood can make peace of mind an elusive goal, even for the most placid parent. As the search for serenity continues, the following quotations should guide fathers and non-fathers alike.

A thankful heart is not only the greatest
virtue, but the parent of all other virtues.

*Cicero*

Thanksgiving invites God to bestow
a second benefit.

*Robert Herrick*

God has two dwellings: one in heaven,
and the other in a meek and thankful heart.

*Izaak Walton*

Contentment is a pearl of great price,
and whoever procures it at the expense
of ten thousand desires makes a wise and
happy purchase.

*John Balguy*

Order your soul; reduce your wants; live in charity; associate in Christian community; obey the laws; trust in Providence.

*St. Augustine*

If there is to be any peace, it will come through being, not having.

*Henry Miller*

Thinking about interior peace destroys interior peace. The patient who constantly feels his pulse is not getting any better.

*Hubert van Zeller*

In truth, to attain inner peace, one must be willing to pass through the contrary to peace.

*Swami Brahmananda*

Peace is not the absence of conflict, but the presence of God no matter what the conflict.

*Unknown*

The peace is won by accompanying God into battle.

*Eivind Josef Berggrav*

Little minds have little worries. Big minds have no room for worries.

*Ralph Waldo Emerson*

As a cure for worrying, work is better than whiskey.

*Thomas Alva Edison*

Sadness is almost never
anything but a form
of fatigue.

*André Gide*

The happiness of man consists in life.
And life is labor.

*Leo Tolstoy*

The busiest man is the happiest man.

*Sir Theodore Martin*

When troubles arise, wise men go
to their work.

*Elbert Hubbard*

A well-spent day brings happy sleep.

*Leonardo da Vinci*

# How unhappy is he who cannot forgive himself.

*Publilius Syrus*

If we have not peace within ourselves,
it is in vain to seek it from outward sources.

*La Rochefoucauld*

Nothing can bring you peace but yourself.

*Ralph Waldo Emerson*

Most folks are about as happy
as they make up their minds to be.

*Abraham Lincoln*

Happiness belongs to those who are sufficient
unto themselves.

*Arthur Schopenhauer*

Forgiving those who hurt us is the key
to personal peace.

*G. Weatherly*

No man is more cheated than the selfish man.

*Henry Ward Beecher*

When a man has pity on all living creatures
then only is he noble.

*Buddha*

Only the just man enjoys peace of mind.

*Epictetus*

Living well and beautifully and justly are all one thing.

*Socrates*

Trouble knocked at the door but, hearing a laugh within, hurried away.

*Poor Richard's Almanac*

A contented mind is the greatest blessing
a man can enjoy in this life.

*Joseph Addison*

Having the fewest wants, I am nearest
to the gods.

*Socrates*

Contentment consists not in multiplying
wealth but in subtracting desires.

*Thomas Fuller*

Abundance consists not so much in material
possessions but in an uncovetous spirit.

*John Selden*

Better one hand full and peace of mind,
than both fists full and toil that is chasing
the wind.

*Ecclesiastes 4:6*

I have learned, in whatever state I am,
therewith to be content.

*Philippians 4:11*

Peace is to man what yeast is to dough.

*Old Saying*

Troubles are often the tools by which God
fashions us for better things.

*Henry Ward Beecher*

There may be those on earth who dress
better or eat better, but those who enjoy
the peace of God sleep better.

*L. Thomas Holdcraft*

When we believe that God is Father, we also believe that such a father's hand will never cause his child a needless tear. We may not understand life any better, but we will not resent life any longer.

*William Barclay*

The one serious conviction that a man should have is that nothing is to be taken too seriously.

*Samuel Butler*

A man travels the world over in search of what he needs and returns home to find it.

*George Moore*

# 9

# Life

Henry James advised, "Live all you can; it's a mistake not to. It doesn't so much matter what you do, so long as you have your life. If you haven't had that, what have you had?"

A father's job is to help his children understand that life should be savored, not squandered. It was Bishop Fulton J. Sheen who observed, "Time is so precious that God deals it out only second by second." In this chapter, we consider the short interval between birth and death and how best to spend it.

One life — a little gleam of time
between two eternities.

*Thomas Carlyle*

The present will not long endure.

*Pindar*

Is not life a hundred times too short for us
to bore ourselves?

*Friedrich Nietzsche*

Life is short, art long, opportunity fleeting,
experience treacherous, judgment difficult.

*Hippocrates*

Real generosity toward the future consists
in giving all to what is present.

*Albert Camus*

Life is what happens to us while we are
making other plans.

*Thomas La Mance*

The art of living is more like wrestling
than dancing.

*Marcus Aurelius*

Life is not a problem to be solved
but a reality to be experienced.

*Søren Kierkegaard*

Life is like playing a violin in public
and learning the instrument as one goes on.

*Samuel Butler*

Life is a series of collisions with the future;
it is not a sum of what we have been
but what we yearn to be.

*José Ortega y Gasset*

Life is a language in which certain truths
are conveyed to us; if we could learn them in
some other way, we should not live.

*Arthur Schopenhauer*

The great use of life is to spend it
for something that will outlast it.

*William James*

As I grow to understand life less and less,
I learn to live it more and more.

*Jules Renard*

Life ain't no dress rehearsal!

*Mark Twain*

Life can only be understood backwards
but must be lived forward.

*Søren Kierkegaard*

Living is a constant process of deciding
what we are going to do.

*José Ortega y Gasset*

Life is a great bundle of little things.

*Oliver Wendell Holmes, Sr.*

Growth is the only evidence of life.

*John Henry Cardinal Newman*

The best way to prepare for life
is to begin to live.

*Elbert Hubbard*

Life is the art of drawing sufficient conclusions
from insufficient premises.

*Samuel Butler*

The tragedy of life is what dies inside a man
while he lives.

*Albert Schweitzer*

The game of life is not so much in holding
a good hand as playing a poor hand well.

*H. T. Leslie*

Our life is what our thoughts make it.

*Marcus Aurelius*

If you want to die happily, learn to live.

*Celio Calcagnini*

He who has a "why"
to live for can bear with
almost any "how".

*Friedrich Nietzsche*

To cheat oneself of love
is the most terrible deception.
*Søren Kierkegaard*

Life is a romantic business,
but you have to make the romance.
*Oliver Wendell Holmes, Sr.*

Life is the flower of which love is the honey.
*Victor Hugo*

Passion makes all things alive and significant.
*Ralph Waldo Emerson*

We have no more right to consume happiness
without producing it than to consume wealth
without producing it.

*George Bernard Shaw*

He only is advancing in life whose heart is
getting softer, whose blood warmer,
whose brain quicker, whose spirit is entering
into living peace.

*John Ruskin*

To live is not to live for one's self alone;
let us help one another.

*Menander*

When people are serving,
life is no longer meaningless.

*John Gardner*

The man who has no inner life is the slave
of his surroundings.

*Henri Frédéric Amiel*

Every man's life is a plan of God.

*Horace Bushnell*

Life is short. Make the most of the present.

*Marcus Aurelius*

Life is 10% what you
make it and 90%
how you take it.

*Irving Berlin*

Thank God every morning when you get up
that you have something to do that day which
must be done, whether you like it or not.

*Charles Kingsley*

A life spent making mistakes is not only
more honorable but also more useful
than a life spent doing nothing.

*George Bernard Shaw*

Were it offered to my choice, I should have
no objections to a repetition of the same life
from its beginning, only asking the advantages
authors have in a second edition to correct
some faults of the first.

*Ben Franklin*

He who asks of life nothing but the
improvement of his own nature is less liable
than anyone else to miss and waste life.

*Henri Frédéric Amiel*

# 10

## Success

Phillips Brooks observed, "To find his place and fill it is success for a man." But finding one's place is not always easy. Sometimes, a little fatherly advice can help.

The British writer George Bernard Shaw defined success by saying, "This is the true joy in life: being used for a purpose recognized by yourself as a mighty one." If you're interested in ways to recognize your place and successfully fill it, read on. The following quotations provide advice that any father would be proud to call his own.

The destiny of man is in his own soul.

*Herodotus*

Ruin and recovery are both from within.

*Epictetus*

Success abides longer among men
when it is planted by the hand of God.

*Pindar*

He who would climb the ladder must begin
at the bottom.

*English Proverb*

You always pass failure on the way to success.

*Mickey Rooney*

It takes twenty years
to make an overnight
success.

*Eddie Cantor*

A man is only as good as what he loves.

*Saul Bellow*

Why should we be in such desperate haste
to succeed, and in such desperate
enterprises? If a man does not keep pace
with his companions, perhaps it is because
he hears a different drummer.

*Henry David Thoreau*

Being humble involves the willingness
to be reckoned a failure in everyone's sight
but God's.

*Roy M. Pearson*

Success is to be measured not by wealth,
power, or fame, but by the ratio between what
a man is and what he might be.

*H. G. Wells*

# Work to become, not acquire.

*Elbert Hubbard*

He who has never failed somewhere,
    that man cannot be great.

*Herman Melville*

There is no failure except in no longer trying.

*Elbert Hubbard*

Failure is only the opportunity to begin again,
    more intelligently.

*Henry Ford*

The way to success is to double
    your failure rate.

*Thomas J. Watson*

It is hard to fail, but it is worse never to have tried to succeed.

*Theodore Roosevelt*

When you blunder, blunder forward.

*Thomas Alva Edison*

Constant effort and frequent mistakes are the stepping-stones of genius.

*Elbert Hubbard*

How to succeed — try hard enough.
How to fail — try too hard.

*Malcolm Forbes*

Whatever you do, do it with purpose;
  do it thoroughly, not superficially.

*Lord Chesterfield*

Success consists in the climb.

*Elbert Hubbard*

If you wish to succeed in life,
  make perseverance your bosom friend,
experience your wise counselor, caution your
elder brother, and hope your guardian genius.

*Joseph Addison*

Take the obvious, add a cupful of brains,
a generous pinch of imagination, a bucketful
of courage and daring, stir well and bring it
  to a boil.

*Bernard Baruch*

If A equals success, then the formula is
A equals X plus Y plus Z. X is work. Y is play.
Z is keep your mouth shut.

*Albert Einstein*

The secret to success in life is for a man to
be ready for his opportunity when it comes.

*Benjamin Disraeli*

My formula for success?
Rise early, work late, strike oil.

*J. Paul Getty*

I can give you a six-word formula for success:
Think things through — then follow through.

*Eddie Rickenbacker*

Great minds have purposes,
       others have wishes.

*Washington Irving*

The man without a purpose is like a ship
      without a rudder — a waif, a nothing,
          a no man.

*Thomas Carlyle*

Try not to become a man of success
       but rather a man of value.

*Albert Einstein*

Life offers no assurances, so you might as
well do what you're really passionate about.

*Jim Carrey*

Whenever you see a successful business,
someone once made a courageous decision.

*Peter Drucker*

Do your work with your whole heart, and you
will succeed — there is so little competition.

*Elbert Hubbard*

Einstein's three rules of work:
1. Out of clutter find simplicity.
2. From discord make harmony.
3. In the middle of difficulty lies opportunity.

If a man loves the labor of any trade,
apart from any question of success or fame,
the Gods have called him.

*Robert Louis Stevenson*

I look on that man as happy who,
  when there is question of success,
    looks to his work for a reply.

*Ralph Waldo Emerson*

Success is relative. It is what we can make
  of the mess we have made of things.

*T. S. Eliot*

Greatness is not found in possessions,
  power, position or prestige. It is discovered
in goodness, humility, service and character.

*William Ward*

Success has nothing to do with what you
    gain in life or accomplish for yourself.
      It is what you do for others.

*Danny Thomas*

# 11

# Memories

Memories of our fathers are priceless possessions; in this chapter, a few notable figures share theirs. Republican Howard Baker once observed, "My father had a profound impact on me in a way I don't think I could ever explain." Democrat Mario Cuomo remembered his father by saying, "I talk and talk and talk, and I haven't taught people in 50 years what my father taught by example in one week." Mr. Baker and Mr. Cuomo thus proved once and for all that admiration for fathers is something upon which even Republicans and Democrats can agree.

Growing up as a preacher's son was tough because the other kids figured you had money. We didn't. What we did have was a daddy with tremendous integrity, a genuine Christian, and a mother with boundless love.

*Sinbad*

My parents were strict, disciplined, and oriented toward education. My father worked very hard to build a good life for us. My mother loved to cook and work and laugh.

*José Canseco*

I had a wonderful, happy childhood. I think my parents liked to inspire creativity, winningness, productivity in their children. It mattered to them what we thought, felt, and did. Our happiness was important to them.

*John Travolta*

When my mother needed someone 24 years ago, Phil Harrison was the man. He is my dad. He's the one who raised me and made me what I am today.

*Shaquille O'Neal, on his stepfather*

My father produced Shakespeare festivals throughout Ohio when I was growing up. I played more murdered princes, mustard seeds, and fairies and elves than I could count.

*John Lithgow*

My father had the poorest lemon ranch in California, I can assure you. He sold it before they found oil on it.

*Richard M. Nixon*

I never thought of us as rich or poor. We always had enough. We never had a car and we didn't have a radio. My father's little motor-bike was the family transportation. I never thought about what we didn't have; I am still that way. All around me I see people making themselves unhappy with such thoughts.

*Luciano Pavarotti*

It's hard for me to talk about a legacy or a mystique. It's my family — the fact that there have been difficulties and hardships makes us closer.

*John F. Kennedy, Jr.*

My dad ended up selling vacuum cleaners, and my mom got a job as a secretary. They never got rich and they never got famous, but they showed me that you do things for a purpose.

*Julia Roberts*

Our relationship was very solid, with a tremendous amount of discipline but also a lot of respect — respect enough to know the difference between father and child.

*Arnold Schwarzenegger*

Pop didn't just teach me golf. He taught me discipline.

*Arnold Palmer*

My father was not a failure.
After all, he was the father
of a president of the
United States.

*Harry S. Truman*

Pride in one's father
reinforces love.

*Margaret Truman*

Our father, while he lived, had cast a
magic over everything. He held his love up
over us like an umbrella and kept off the
troubles.

*Mary Lavin*

I watched a small man with thick calluses on
both hands work 15 to 16 hours a day. I saw
him once literally bleed from the bottoms of
his feet, a man who came here uneducated,
alone, unable to speak the language, who
taught me all I needed to know about faith
and hard work by the simple eloquence
of his example.

*Mario Cuomo*

He was a man who for years had, to my
naturally prejudiced mind, set a splendid
example — not just to me but to the world —
of irresistible optimism and vitality,
and a love of all life could offer.

*Douglas Fairbanks, Jr.*

It doesn't matter who my father was; it matters who I remember he was.

*Anne Sexton*

I wanted to be like my father, but not *exactly* like him. It's tough growing up in the shadow of a national monument.

*Jane Fonda*

I don't think I've been a particularly good father, but I've been lucky in the quality of my kids.

*Henry Fonda*

When a child, my dreams rode on your wishes,
I was your son, high on your horse,
My mind atop whipped by the lashes
Of your rhetoric, windy of course.

*Stephen Foster*

Everyone had their chores. We all had to eat
together every meal. Mom cooked, we helped,
while we waited for Dad to come home
from work. It was like the American Dream.
My family was almost perfect. I was very lucky.

*Reggie Miller*


He was a gentleman and a gentle man.
My father was sweet, kind, and good-hearted.
He loved his family and spent as much time
as he could with us.

*Natalie Cole, on her father Nat King Cole*


He gave me some valuable things: he gave me
fighting blood, which I needed.

*Tennessee Williams*

# My father saved my life.

*Oprah Winfrey*

# Sources

# About the Author

Criswell Freeman is a Doctor of Clinical Psychology living in Nashville, Tennessee. He is the author of *When Life Throws You a Curveball, Hit It* and numerous books in the Wisdom Series published by WALNUT GROVE PRESS.

Dr. Freeman's Wisdom Books chronicle memorable quotations in an easy-to-read style. The series provides inspiring, thoughtful and humorous messages from entertainers, athletes, scientists, politicians, clerics, writers and renegades, with each title focusing on a particular region or area of special interest. Combining his passion for quotations with extensive training in psychology, Freeman revisits timeless themes such as perseverance, courage, love, forgiveness and faith.

Dr. Freeman is also the host of *Wisdom Made in America*, a nationally syndicated radio program.

# The Wisdom Series
*by Dr. Criswell Freeman*

## Regional Titles

| | |
|---|---|
| Wisdom Made in America | ISBN 1-887655-07-7 |
| The Book of Southern Wisdom | ISBN 0-9640955-3-X |
| The Wisdom of the Midwest | ISBN 1-887655-17-4 |
| The Wisdom of the West | ISBN 1-887655-31-X |
| The Book of Texas Wisdom | ISBN 0-9640955-8-0 |
| The Book of Florida Wisdom | ISBN 0-9640955-9-9 |
| The Book of California Wisdom | ISBN 1-887655-14-X |
| The Book of New York Wisdom | ISBN 1-887655-16-6 |
| The Book of New England Wisdom | ISBN 1-887655-15-8 |

## Sports Titles

| | |
|---|---|
| The Golfer's Book of Wisdom | ISBN 0-9640955-6-4 |
| The Putter Principle | ISBN 1-887655-39-5 |
| The Golfer's Guide to Life | ISBN 1-887655-38-7 |
| The Wisdom of Women's Golf | ISBN 1-887655-82-4 |
| The Book of Football Wisdom | ISBN 1-887655-18-2 |
| The Wisdom of Southern Football | ISBN 0-9640955-7-2 |
| The Book of Stock Car Wisdom | ISBN 1-887655-12-3 |
| The Wisdom of Old-Time Baseball | ISBN 1-887655-08-5 |
| The Book of Basketball Wisdom | ISBN 1-887655-32-8 |
| The Fisherman's Guide to Life | ISBN 1-887655-30-1 |
| The Tennis Lover's Guide to Life | ISBN 1-887655-36-0 |

## Special People Titles

| | |
|---|---|
| Mothers Are Forever | ISBN 1-887655-76-X |
| Fathers Are Forever | ISBN 1-887655-77-8 |
| Friends Are Forever | ISBN 1-887655-78-6 |
| The Teachers' Book of Wisdom | ISBN 1-887655-80-8 |
| The Graduates' Book of Wisdom | ISBN 1-887655-81-6 |
| The Guide to Better Birthdays | ISBN 1-887655-35-2 |
| Get Well Soon...If Not Sooner | ISBN 1-887655-79-4 |
| The Wisdom of the Heart | ISBN 1-887655-34-4 |

## Special Interest Titles

| | |
|---|---|
| The Book of Country Music Wisdom | ISBN 0-9640955-1-3 |
| Old-Time Country Wisdom | ISBN 1-887655-26-3 |
| The Wisdom of Old-Time Television | ISBN 1-887655-64-6 |
| The Book of Cowboy Wisdom | ISBN 1-887655-41-7 |
| The Gardener's Guide to Life | ISBN 1-887655-40-9 |
| The Salesman's Book of Wisdom | ISBN 1-887655-83-2 |
| Minutes from the Great Women's Coffee Club (by Angela Beasley) | ISBN 1-887655-33-6 |